T0039892

CAT SELFIES

BY M.D. MULLINS

A POST HILL PRESS BOOK
ISBN: 978-1-64293-295-9

Cat Selfies
© 2021 by M.D. Mullins
All Rights Reserved

No part of this book may be reproduced, stored in a retrieval system, or transmitted by any means without the written permission of the author and publisher.

Post Hill Press
New York ▪ Nashville
posthillpress.com

Published in the United States of America
Printed in Singapore
1 2 3 4 5 6 7 8 9 10

DEDICATION

To those who rescue, foster and adopt animals in need.
All cats featured were rescues. Many still need homes.

SPECIAL THANKS

Regina Carrone, Catopia Cat Rescue
Kelly Parker, Chicago Cat Rescue
Lana Vitsup, Zani's Furry Friends
Theresa LaBianca, Sean Casey Animal Rescue
Roberta Giordano, Bobbi and the Strays Pet Rescue
Nora Wood & Kitti Brady, Anjellicle Cats Rescue
Maria Rozos & Michelle Portlock, Infinite Hope
Jennilyn Carson, East Harlem Kitty Rescue
Eva Prokop & Jenna Jane McMaster, Whiskers-A-GoGo
Sara Cameron & Ken Salerno, Calling All Cats Rescue
Maria Conlon, Give Me Shelter
Lusana Masrur, North Country Animal League
Catherine Snyder, Second Chance Animal Center
Debbie Edge & Lisa Bourgault, Jake's Place Cat Rescue
Jane Warshaw, Animal Welfare Warrior
Lisa Alexander, Animal Welfare Warrior
Maria Milito, Animal Welfare Warrior
Susan Richard, Animal Welfare Warrior
Bunny Hofberg, Animal Welfare Warrior
Esther Koslow, Animal Welfare Warrior

Smile, life is beautiful.

DID YOU KNOW

HAVING A CAT CAN REDUCE YOUR RISK OF HEART ATTACK OR STROKE BY A THIRD. STUDIES HAVE SHOWN CAT COMPANIONSHIP RELIEVES ANXIETY AND STRESS.

Who do I gotta knead to
get out of this joint?

DID YOU KNOW

RESCUE ORGANIZATIONS HAVE PARTNERED WITH CORRECTIONAL FACILITIES TO ALLOW SELECT INMATES TO FOSTER SHELTER CATS. THE PROGRAMS ARE SAID TO ALLEVIATE SHELTER OVERCROWDING WHILE HELPING TO REHABILITATE THE INCARCERATED.

So, you're 40 and single?

DID YOU KNOW

WHILE CAT OWNERSHIP IS TRADITIONALLY ASSOCIATED WITH WOMEN, A NEW STUDY FINDS THAT AMONG MILLENNIALS IN THE UNITED STATES, MEN DOMINATE.

I didn't bring you bad luck.
Your life already sucked.

DID YOU KNOW

IN CONTRAST TO THE BACKWARD VIEW THAT BLACK CATS ARE BAD LUCK, IN ENGLAND THESE MINI PANTHERS ARE ASSOCIATED WITH GOOD FORTUNE. ALSO, SAILORS HAVE HISTORICALLY KEPT BLACK CATS FOR SAFE TRAVEL.

Pass the catnip.

DID YOU KNOW

ABOUT ONE THIRD OF CATS HAVE NO REACTION TO CATNIP. THESE CATS LACK THE GENE NECESSARY FOR CATNIP STIMULATION. KITTENS LESS THAN THREE MONTHS OF AGE ALSO DO NOT RESPOND TO CATNIP.

I go into survival mode when tickled.

DID YOU KNOW

A THIRD OF THOSE BIT BY A CAT IN THE UNITED STATES REQUIRE MEDICAL ATTENTION. WHILE DOG BITES ARE MORE COMMON, CAT BITES CAN OFTEN CAUSE INFECTION.

Lost my ears, retained my beauty.

DID YOU KNOW

A CAT'S EXTERNAL EAR ROTATES UP TO 180 DEGREES ALLOWING IT TO HEAR THE FAINTEST OF SOUNDS. CATS CAN ALSO HEAR AT HIGHER FREQUENCIES THAN DOGS.

So tell me again why

DID YOU KNOW

KITTY LITTER,
AS WE KNOW IT TODAY,
WAS INVENTED BY
ENTREPRENEUR
ED LOWE
IN 1947.
IT IS NOW A
$2 BILLION INDUSTRY

Nobody's perfect. But I'm close.

DID YOU KNOW

NEARLY ALL
TORTOISESHELL CATS
ARE FEMALE.
IN IRISH FOLKLORE
THEY BRING GOOD LUCK.

Fall asleep, I dare you.

DID YOU KNOW

DESPITE WHAT MANY BELIEVE, CATS DO NOT HOLD GRUDGES. BAD BEHAVIOR IS TYPICALLY A RESULT OF STRESS THE CAT IS FEELING AND NOT THEIR DECISION TO EXACT REVENGE, BEHAVIORISTS CLAIM.

Wait, a bath involves water?

DID YOU KNOW

WHILE MANY CATS HAVE AN AVERSION TO WATER, CERTAIN BREEDS, SUCH AS THE TURKISH VAN, ARE KNOWN FOR HAVING AN H_2O AFFINITY AND HAVE BEEN NICKNAMED 'THE SWIMMING CATS.'

Tastes like chicken.

DID YOU KNOW

LINEAR FOREIGN BODIES, SUCH AS THREAD, STRING AND RIBBON, ARE THE MOST COMMON CAUSE OF INTESTINAL OBSTRUCTION IN CATS, AND CAN LEAD TO SERIOUS INTERNAL DAMAGE, EVEN DEATH. CATS MUST BE SUPERVISED WHEN PLAYING WITH SUCH MATERIALS.

My father was a werewolf.

DID YOU KNOW

A CALIFORNIA CAT NAMED SOPHIE SMITH HOLDS THE RECORD FOR LONGEST HAIR WITH A SINGLE STRAND MEASURING JUST SHY OF 11 INCHES.

Mickey, you're mine.

DID YOU KNOW

A SINGLE CAT IS CREDITED WITH HAVING KILLED 28,899 MICE. THE CAT, NOT PICTURED, WAS A LONG-HAIRED TORTOISESHELL NAMED TOWSER AND HER DOMAIN WAS THE GLENTURRET DISTILLERY IN SCOTLAND. SHE LIVED 24 YEARS.

Best friends always have your back.

DID YOU KNOW

A FEMALE KITTEN CAN BECOME PREGNANT AT 4 MONTHS OF AGE. WITH GESTATION LASTING 63 TO 65 DAYS, A KITTEN CAN HAVE HER OWN LITTER AT 6 MONTHS OF AGE. IT'S IMPORTANT TO SPAY AND NEUTER.

Is the bear still following me?

DID YOU KNOW

IT IS NOT UNCOMMON FOR CATS TO FEAR INANIMATE OBJECTS THAT LACK FAMILIARITY. AS FOR THOSE WHO FEAR CATS, THEY SUFFER FROM AILUROPHOBIA.

My wingman.

DID YOU KNOW

ATTACKS BY CATS ARE AMONG THE MOST COMMON CAUSE OF BAT CASUALTIES.

You work 60 hours weekly, I sleep 16 hours daily. You own me?

DID YOU KNOW

CATS ON AVERAGE SLEEP 70% OF THE DAY TO CONSERVE ENERGY. HARDWIRED TO HUNT, CATS IN THE WILD REQUIRE EVERY BIT OF ENERGY TO CATCH THEIR PREY WHETHER THAT BE A BIRD, MOUSE OR IN THIS CASE, A FEATHER TEASER.

Have a seat, we were expecting you.

DID YOU KNOW

THE LENGTH OF A KITTEN'S WHISKERS AND THE WIDTH OF THEIR BODY ARE APPROXIMATELY EQUAL AS KITTENS OFTEN RELY ON THEIR WHISKERS TO NAVIGATE INITIALLY. SECURELY CONNECTED TO THE CAT'S NERVOUS SYSTEM, WHISKERS SHOULD NEVER BE CUT.

One eye. One heart. All yours.

DID YOU KNOW

CATS SMILE BY SQUINTING AT US. SLOW BLINKING, HEAD-BUNTING AND KNEADING ARE OTHER SIGNS THAT YOUR CAT IS CONTENT WITH YOU. WHILE CATS CAN SMILE, BEHAVIORISTS SAY SUCH EXPRESSIONS ARE NOT A SIGN OF AFFECTION.

Life is uncertain. Eat dessert first.

DID YOU KNOW

CATS DO NOT
HAVE A SWEET TOOTH.
CATS LACK CERTAIN TASTE
RECEPTOR PROTEINS ON
THEIR TONGUE,
MAKING IT IMPOSSIBLE
FOR THEM TO TASTE SWEETS.
CATS ARE THE ONLY
KNOWN MAMMAL
UNABLE TO TASTE SWEETS.

Always bring your slay game.

DID YOU KNOW

MALE CATS CAN MOUNT A FEMALE IN HEAT IN AS LITTLE AS 16 SECONDS. ON AVERAGE, MATING CAN TAKE ANYWHERE FROM ONE TO NINE MINUTES AND ONCE COMPLETE, THE MALE CAT ABANDONS THE FEMALE.

Wanna hear a scary story?

DID YOU KNOW

IN JAPANESE FOLKLORE, CATS CAN MORPH INTO SUPERNATURAL, BLOOD-THIRSTY CREATURES KNOWN AS THE BAKENEKO OR 'GHOST CAT.' DESPITE THE INTENSE STARE, THE CAT PICTURED IS NOT A BAKENEKO AND IS QUITE FRIENDLY.

Your tuna or your life.

DID YOU KNOW

TOO MUCH TUNA CAN CAUSE MALNUTRITION AND TOXICITY IN CATS. TUNA LACKS THE NUTRIENTS CATS REQUIRE IN THEIR DIET AND CAN LEAD TO MERCURY POISONING.

Sassy, classy, and a bit bad-assy.

DID YOU KNOW

CATS MARK YOU AS THEIR TERRITORY BY RUBBING AGAINST YOU WITH THEIR SCENT GLANDS. CONSIDER YOURSELF LUCKY, CATS ALSO USE URINE TO MARK THEIR TERRITORY.

Let my eyes do the talking.

DID YOU KNOW

THE GLIMMER WE SEE
IN A CAT'S EYE AT NIGHT
IS A RAY OF SUNLIGHT
STORED FOR SAFEKEEPING
BY THE SUN GOD RA
'TIL DAY RETURNS,
SO SAY THE
ANCIENT EGYPTIANS.

This is me surprised.

DID YOU KNOW

300,000 MUMMIFIED CATS WERE FOUND IN 1888 IN AN ANCIENT EGYPTIAN CEMETERY. THE CAT MUMMIES WERE STRIPPED AND SOLD AS FERTILIZER TO FARMERS IN ENGLAND.

Pedicure time.

DID YOU KNOW

DECLAWING A CAT IS AN AMPUTATION OF THE CAT'S BONE THAT CAN CAUSE LASTING PHYSICAL PROBLEMS, WHILE PROVIDING NO MEDICAL BENEFIT. INSTEAD, CATS SHOULD HAVE THEIR NAILS TRIMMED EVERY 2 TO 4 WEEKS.

Our ears light-up when we ignore you

DID YOU KNOW

APPROXIMATELY 80% OF ORANGE TABBIES ARE MALE. THE REASON: FEMALE ORANGE TABBIES REQUIRE BOTH PARENTS TO HAVE AN ORANGE COAT WHEREAS MALES ONLY NEED THEIR MOTHER TO HAVE THE ORANGE GENE.

Is the zombie apocalypse over?

DID YOU KNOW

DOMESTIC CATS
CAN REACH A SPEED OF
NEARLY 30 MPH
WITHIN SECONDS.
THE SPEED LASTS ONLY
IN SHORT SPURTS,
WHICH IS KEY
TO CATCHING PREY
AND
OUTRUNNING ZOMBIES.

Can I spend all 9 lives with you?

DID YOU KNOW

MORRIS THE CAT,
THE 9LIVES BRAND
OF CAT FOOD MASCOT,
WAS A RESCUE CAT
ADOPTED
FROM AN ILLINOIS
ANIMAL SHELTER.

I'm ready for my closeup.

DID YOU KNOW

MORE THAN TWO-THIRDS OF BLUE-EYED WHITE CATS ARE DEAF IN AT LEAST ONE EAR. ABOUT 20% OF WHITE CATS WITH NONBLUE EYES ARE ALSO DEAF.

Cuddle time?

DID YOU KNOW

THE HORMONE OXYTOCIN IS RELEASED WHEN ONE STROKES A CAT. THE SAME HORMONE IS ALSO ASSOCIATED WITH MATERNAL ATTACHMENT AND SEXUAL PLEASURE.

WARNING: You may fall in love with me

DID YOU KNOW

OUTGOING CATS HAVE A BETTER CHANCE OF GETTING ADOPTED. IN CONTRAST, A DOG'S APPEARANCE, MORE SO THAN THEIR BEHAVIOR, IS SAID TO PLAY A GREATER ROLE IN ITS ADOPTION.

It's not me. It's you.

DID YOU KNOW

CATS PERCEIVE HUMANS TO BE BIG, DUMB CATS, SO SAYS BRITISH ANTHROZOOLOGIST JOHN BRADSHAW, WHO HAS BEEN STUDYING CATS FOR 30 YEARS.

Give me a scotch, I am starving.

DID YOU KNOW

A TABLESPOON OF ALCOHOL CAN PUT A CAT IN A COMA. CATS SHOULD NEVER CONSUME ALCOHOL, AS EXPOSURE HAS RESULTED IN BRAIN AND LIVER DAMAGE, AS WELL AS DEATH.

You talking to me?

DID YOU KNOW

DOMESTIC CATS SHARE MORE THAN 95% OF THEIR DNA WITH TIGERS. HUMANS SHARE ABOUT 90% OF THEIR DNA WITH DOMESTIC CATS.

I do a thing called what I want.

DID YOU KNOW

WHILE A CAT OFTEN RECOGNIZES THEIR OWNER'S VOICE, THEY TYPICALLY CHOOSE TO IGNORE IT. RESEARCHERS ATTRIBUTE THIS DISMISSIVENESS TO THEIR EVOLUTIONARY HISTORY.

First spa day.

DID YOU KNOW

THE MOST PROLIFIC CAT ON RECORD WAS A TABBY FROM TEXAS. NAMED DUSTY, SHE GAVE BIRTH TO 420 KITTENS IN HER LIFETIME. DUSTY'S FIRST LITTER WAS IN JUNE OF 1952 AND CONSISTED OF JUST ONE KITTEN.

Ever been devoured by a blanket?

DID YOU KNOW

MUCH LIKE
HUMAN FINGERPRINTS,
EACH CAT'S NOSE PRINT,
WITH ITS PATTERN OF
RIDGES AND BUMPS,
IS UNIQUE.

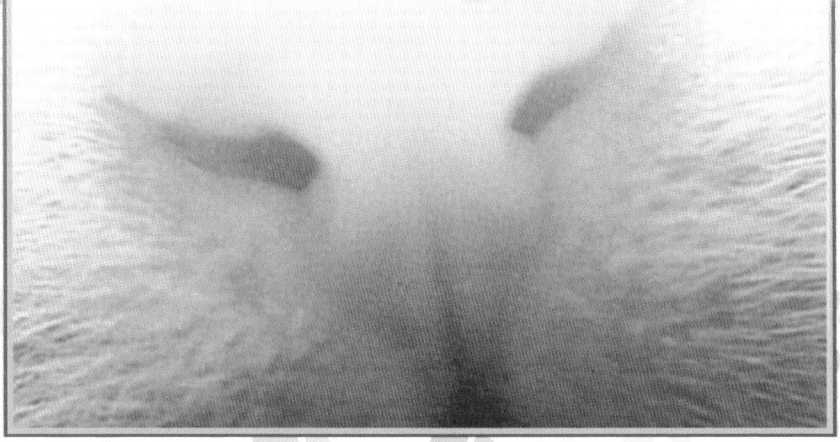

I taught Pele everything he knows.

DID YOU KNOW

AN ADOPTED CAT
NAMED DIDGA,
NOT PICTURED,
HOLDS THE
GUINNESS RECORD
FOR MOST TRICKS
PERFORMED IN A MINUTE.
FROM ROLLING OVER
TO SKATEBOARD JUMPING,
DIDGA PERFORMED
20 TRICKS IN 60 SECONDS.

Catnip every minute.

DID YOU KNOW

CATS SENSITIVE TO THE EFFECTS OF CATNIP MELLOW OUT WHEN THEY INGEST THE HERB, AND BECOME PLAYFUL WHEN THEY SMELL IT. FOR HUMANS, CATNIP HAS A CALMING EFFECT.

You sleep on the floor tonight, human

DID YOU KNOW

MORE THAN TWO-THIRDS OF CAT OWNERS SLEEP WITH THEIR CATS. A STUDY FINDS THAT 62% OF ADULTS SLEEP WITH THEIR CATS, WHILE AN ADDITIONAL 13% OF CHILDREN ALSO SLEEP WITH THEIR FELINE COMPANIONS.

When does this story end?

DID YOU KNOW

THE SAME GENE RESPONSIBLE FOR GIVING THE CHEETAH IT'S SPOTS GIVES THE TABBY IT'S STRIPES. IF THE GENE IS MUTATED, THE STRIPES WILL APPEAR BLOTCHED ON THE TABBY.

Kitten today. Panther tomorrow.

DID YOU KNOW

TWENTY-TWO CAT BREEDS
CAN HAVE
SOLID BLACK COATS.
WITH THE RARE EXCEPTION
OF A SABLE-COLORED KITTEN,
THE BOMBAY CAT
IS THE ONLY BREED THAT
IS EXCLUSIVELY BLACK.

We come in every flavor.

DID YOU KNOW

A SINGLE LITTER OF KITTENS CAN HAVE MULTIPLE FATHERS. WHILE IN HEAT, A FEMALE CAN MATE WITH SEVERAL MALES, RESULTING IN DIFFERENT TOM CATS FERTILIZING DIFFERENT EGGS.

Wake up mom. Wake up.

DID YOU KNOW

MOTHER CATS OFTEN COMMUNICATE WITH THEIR KITTENS THROUGH A UNIQUE SOUND KNOWN AS A CHIRRUP. AS ADULTS, CATS USE THE SAME SOUND WITH HUMANS THEY LOVE AND TRUST.

The best cats are a bit crazy.

DID YOU KNOW

A CONNECTICUT CAT NAMED LEWIS WAS PLACED UNDER HOUSE ARREST IN 2006. THE SAME CAT HAD A RESTRAINING ORDER FILED AGAINST HIM FOR ALLEGEDLY ATTACKING LOCALS. LEWIS, NOT PICTURED, IS NOW AN INDOOR CAT.

If we fit, we sit.

DID YOU KNOW

CATS HAVE FREE-FLOATING CLAVICLE BONES. THIS ALLOWS THEM TO FIT INTO THE TIGHTEST OF SPACES AND CONTORT THEIR BODY WITH EASE.

I'm Prada. You're Nada.

DID YOU KNOW

U.S. CONSUMERS
SPENT MORE THAN
$72 BILLION
ON THEIR PETS IN 2018.
IN 1994, U.S. CONSUMERS
SPENT $17 BILLION
ON THEIR PETS.

Don't swim with sharks.

When can we swim with more sharks?

PHOTO CREDIT INDEX

1. Photo by Kelly Parker, Chicago Cat Rescue Volunteer Photographer (www.chicagocatrescue.org/) / (773) 203-0215
2. Kate Devlin, 'Owning a cat 'cuts stroke risk by third,' The Telegraph, March 19 2008
3. Photo by Lana Vitsup, Zani's Furry Friends Volunteer Web Master/Designer, Photographer, Writer, Instagram Manager (https://zanisfurryfriends.org/)
4. Nicole Hamilton, 'Innovative prison program gives cats (and inmates) a bright future,' BestFriends.org, June 27 2016
5. Photo by Kelly Parker, Chicago Cat Rescue Volunteer Photographer (www.chicagocatrescue.org/) / (773) 203-0215
6. Statista.com, 'Cat and dog ownership among U.S. Millennials, by gender 2017' (www.statista.com/statistics/831452/pet-ownership-united-states-millennials-cat-dog/)
7. Rescued/Adopted Bronx, NY Kitten
8. Louise Hung, '7 Ways Black Cats Bring Good Luck Around the World,' Catster.com, October 29 2018
9. Photo by Staff at North Country Animal League (www.ncal.com)
10. Pam Johnson-Bennett, 'The Catnip Response,' CatBehaviorAssociates.com
11. Photo by Lana Vitsup, Zani's Furry Friends Volunteer Web Master/Designer, Photographer, Writer, Instagram Manager (https://zanisfurryfriends.org/)
12. 'Is a Cat Bite Worse than a Dog Bite?' Animal Medical Center Blog, May 14 2014 (www.amcny.org/blog/2014/05/14/is-a-cat-bite-worse-than-a-dog-bite)
13. Photo by Kelly Parker, Chicago Cat Rescue Volunteer Photographer (www.chicagocatrescue.org/) / (773) 203-0215
14. Jane A. Kelley, '6 Cool Facts About Cat Ears' Catster.com, August 4 2017
15. Photo by Lana Vitsup, Zani's Furry Friends Volunteer Web Master/Designer, Photographer, Writer, Instagram Manager (https://zanisfurryfriends.org/)
16. Daniel A. Gross, 'How Kitty Litter went from happy accident to $2 billion industry,' The Washington Post, February 2 2015
17. Photo by Lisa Bourgault of Fuzzball Photography, Jake's Place Cat Rescue (www.jakesplacecatrescue.org/)

18. Selena Barrientos, '10 Totally Fascinating Facts About Tortoiseshell Cats,' GoodHouseKeeping.com, June 4 2019
19. East Harlem Kitty Rescue / eastharlemkitty@aol.com
20. Marilyn Krieger, 'Your Cat Doesn't "Get Even" With You Through Unwanted Behavior,' Catster.com, March 20 2015
21. Infinite Hope (www.infinitehope.org) / infinitehopeanimalrescue@gmail.com
22. Laura Moss, '9 Cat Breeds That Love Water,' AdventureCats.org, October 19, 2015
23. Photo by Kelly Parker, Chicago Cat Rescue Volunteer Photographer (www.chicagocatrescue.org/) / (773) 203-0215
24. Arnold Plotnick DVM, 'Linear Foreign Bodies in Cats,' ManhattanCats.com
25. Whiskers-A-GoGo (www.whiskers-agogo.org) / whiskersagogo.nyc@gmail.com
26. 'Longest fur on a cat,' (www.guinnessworldrecords.com/world-records/longest-fur-on-a-cat)
27. Photo by Regina Carrone, Catopia Cat Rescue Director (catopiacatrescue.org) / catopiacatrescue@gmail.com
28. 'Greatest mouser' (www.guinnessworldrecords.com/world-records/greatest-mouser/)
29. Photo by Regina Carrone, Catopia Cat Rescue Director (catopiacatrescue.org) / catopiacatrescue@gmail.com
30. Amy Flowers DVM, 'What to Expect When Your Cat Is Pregnant,' Pets.WebMD.com, May 20 2019
31. Anjellicle Cats Rescue (www.AnjellicleCats.com) / info@anjelliclecats.com
32. Maura McAndrew, '8 Common Cat Fears and Anxieties' PetMD.com
33. Whiskers-A-GoGo (www.whiskers-agogo.org) / whiskersagogo.nyc@gmail.com
34. Bat Conservation Trust (www.bats.org.uk/about-bats/threats-to-bats/cat-attacks)
35. Photo by Bridgette Murray, Calling All Cats Rescues Volunteer / cacreventsmgr@gmail.com
36. Jawad Ahmad, 'Cats spend 70% of their lives asleep,' VeterinaryHub.com, June 13 2013
37. Photo by Lana Vitsup, Zani's Furry Friends Volunteer Web Master/Designer, Photographer, Writer, Instagram Manager (https://zanisfurryfriends.org/)
38. Yahaira Cespedes, 'Why Do Cats Have Whiskers?' PetMD.com
39. Photo by Michelle Portlock, Infinite Hope Board VP (www.infinitehope.org) / infinitehopeanimalrescue@gmail.com

40. Ingrid Newkirk, 'Reading Your Cat's Eyes,' PETA.org, September 13 2018 // Charlotte Corney, 'Can cats smile?' ScienceFocus.com
41. East Harlem Kitty Rescue / eastharlemkitty@aol.com
42. David Biello, 'Strange but True: Cats Cannot Taste Sweets,' ScientificAmerican.com, August 16 2007
43. Photo by Regina Carrone, Catopia Cat Rescue Director (catopiacatrescue.org) / catopiacatrescue@gmail.com
44. Beth Asaff, 'Male Cat Behavior Characteristics,' Cats.LoveToKnow.com
45. Anjellicle Cats Rescue (www.AnjellicleCats.com) / info@anjelliclecats.com
46. Alicia McDermott, 'Beware of the Cat: Tales of the Wicked Japanese Bakeneko and Nekomata,' Ancient-Origins.net, November 6 2015
47. Photo by Kelly Parker, Chicago Cat Rescue Volunteer Photographer (www.chicagocatrescue.org/) / (773) 203-0215
48. Amy Flowers, 'Foods Your Cat Should Never Eat,' Pets.WebMD.com, February 27 2018
49. Photo by Kelly Parker, Chicago Cat Rescue Volunteer Photographer (www.chicagocatrescue.org/) / (773) 203-0215
50. Samantha Drake, 'Cat Behavior: Why Do Cats Rub Against You?' PetMD.com
51. Photo by Scott Berliner, Sean Casey Animal Rescue (www.nyanimalrescue.org) / adopt@nyanimalrescue.org
52. Justine Hankins, 'Windows of a cat's soul,' TheGuardian.com, June 27 2003
53. Photo by Staff at North Country Animal League (www.ncal.com) / info@ncal.com
54. Beach Combing, 'Tens of Thousands of Egyptian Mummies in English Soil?' StrangeHistory.net, December 18 2013
55. Photo by Regina Carrone, Catopia Cat Rescue Director (catopiacatrescue.org) / catopiacatrescue@gmail.com
56. 'Declawing cats: Far worse than a manicure' (www.humanesociety.org/resources/declawing-cats-far-worse-manicure)
57. Photo by Rachel Baird, East Harlem Kitty Rescue / eastharlemkitty@aol.com
58. Susan Pi, 'Why Orange Cats Are Usually Male,' CatTime.com
59. Photo by Regina Carrone, Catopia Cat Rescue Director (catopiacatrescue.org) / catopiacatrescue@gmail.com

60. Cameron Stracher, 'Usain Bolt Versus the House Cat,' WSJ.com, August 23 2009
61. Bobbi and the Strays Pet Rescue (www.bobbiandthestrays.org) / info@bobbicares.org
62. 'Hinsdale Humane Society - Home of Morris the Cat,' (https://www.hinsdalehumanesociety.org/about/morris-the-cat)
63. Photo by Regina Carrone, Catopia Cat Rescue Director (catopiacatrescue.org) / catopiacatrescue@gmail.com
64. 'White Cats and Blindness/Deafness,' (https://www.vet.cornell.edu/departments-centers-and-institutes/cornell-feline-health-center/health-information/feline-health-topics/ask-elizabeth-white-cats-and-blindnessdeafness)
65. Photo by Lana Vitsup, Zani's Furry Friends Volunteer Web Master/Designer, Photographer, Writer, Instagram Manager (https://zanisfurryfriends.org/)
66. Tara Green, 'Do Cats Emit Something That Makes You Love Them?' Pets.TheNest.com // 'What Is Oxytocin?' (https://www.psychologytoday.com/us/basics/oxytocin)
67. Photo by Kelly Parker, Chicago Cat Rescue Volunteer Photographer (www.chicagocatrescue.org/) / (773) 203-0215
68. Shaunacy Ferro, '11 Surprising Facts About Cat Adoptions,' MentalFloss.com, June 6 2017
69. East Harlem Kitty Rescue / eastharlemkitty@aol.com
70. Chris Matyszczyk, 'Scientist: Cats think you are just a big, stupid cat,' CNET.com, January 12 2014
71. Photo by Regina Carrone, Catopia Cat Rescue Director (catopiacatrescue.org) / catopiacatrescue@gmail.com
72. 'Human Foods that are Dangerous for Cats,' (https://m.petmd.com/cat/emergency/poisoning-toxicity/e_ct_human_food_poisoning)
73. Photo by Lana Vitsup, Zani's Furry Friends Volunteer Web Master/Designer, Photographer, Writer, Instagram Manager (https://zanisfurryfriends.org/)
74. Tia Ghose, 'House cats and tigers share 95.6 percent of DNA, study reveals,' CSMonitor.com, September 18 2013 // Steven Silz-Carson, 'How much DNA do humans share with cats? What physical and psychological common features do they share?' Quora.com, January 11 2017
75. Photo by Lana Vitsup, Zani's Furry Friends Volunteer Web Master/Designer, Photographer, Writer, Instagram Manager (https://zanisfurryfriends.org/)

76. Rachel Nuwer, 'Cats Recognize Their Owner's Voice But Choose to Ignore It,' Smithsonian.com, December 2 2013
77. Photo by Theresa LaBianca, Sean Casey Animal Rescue (www.nyanimalrescue.org) / adopt@nyanimalrescue.org
78. 'Most prolific cat,' Guinness World Records (www.guinnessworldrecords.com/world-records/most-prolific-cat)
79. Photo by Santana Snyder, Second Chance Animal Rescue Feline Associate (2ndchanceanimalcenter.org) / felineoffice@2ndchanceanimalcenter.org
80. Jane A Kelley, '4 Cool Facts About Cat Noses,' Catster.com, August 9 2017
81. Infinite Hope (www.infinitehope.org) / infinitehopeanimalrescue@gmail.com
82. Phillip Mlynar, '6 Greatest Guinness World Records Starring Cats,' CatTime.com
83. Photo by Regina Carrone, Catopia Cat Rescue Director (catopiacatrescue.org) / catopiacatrescue@gmail.com
84. 'Why cats lose their minds over this perennial herb' (www.humanesociety.org/resources/crazy-catnip)
85. Infinite Hope (www.infinitehope.org) / infinitehopeanimalrescue@gmail.com
86. Judy Molland, '5 Reasons You Should Never Share Your Bed With Your Cat,' Care2.com, February 12 2017
87. Photo by Emilie Chiang, Give Me Shelter Volunteer (www.givemeshelterst.org) / info@givemeshelterst.org
88. Stephanie Pappas, 'Feline Find: How the Tabby Cat Got Its Stripes,' LiveScience.com, September 20 2012
89. Bobbi and the Strays Pet Rescue (www.bobbiandthestrays.org) / info@bobbicares.org
90. Kaitlin Stainbrook, '8 Hair-Raising Facts About Black Cats,' MentalFloss.com, August 17 2018 // 'Bombay Cat' (https://www.purina.com/cats/cat-breeds/bombay)
91. Photo by Regina Carrone, Catopia Cat Rescue Director (catopiacatrescue.org) / catopiacatrescue@gmail.com
92. Betty Lewis, 'How Is It Possible That Kittens Have More Than One Father?' Pets.TheNest.com
93. Photo by Regina Carrone, Catopia Cat Rescue Director (catopiacatrescue.org) / catopiacatrescue@gmail.com
94. Steve Duno, '12 Sounds Cats Make and What They Mean,' ModernCat.com

95. Photo by Kelly Parker, Chicago Cat Rescue Volunteer Photographer (www.chicagocatrescue.org/) / (773) 203-0215

96. Lynne Tuohy, 'Now a Jailbird, Lewis the Cat awaits his Fate,' Courant.com, June 20 2006 // 'Purrfect ending to story of the felonious feline,' NYDailynews.com, July 5 2008

97. Photo by Regina Carrone, Catopia Cat Rescue Director (catopiacatrescue.org) / catopiacatrescue@gmail.com

98. 'Secrets of Animal Acrobats: Why Are Cats So Flexible?' CatCheckup.com, January 30 2019

99. Photo by Regina Carrone, Catopia Cat Rescue Director (catopiacatrescue.org) / catopiacatrescue@gmail.com

100. American Pet Products Association (www.americanpetproducts.org/press_industrytrends.asp)

101/102. Photo by Regina Carrone, Catopia Cat Rescue Director (catopiacatrescue.org) / catopiacatrescue@gmail.com. BACKGROUND: Vitani, the cat pictured, was not rescued from a shark attack; rather she was discovered in a Florida parking lot with a severe leg injury. Vitani's leg was amputated due to the extent of the injury. Thanks to the efforts of Catopia Cat Rescue, Vitani has since been placed in a loving forever home that includes two other tripod (three-legged) cats, one tripod dog, and a special needs dog. In the words of Catopia Director Regina Carrone, "She ended up in the perfect home and is deeply loved."

ABOUT THE AUTHOR

Michael D. Mullins is an award-winning journalist, lifelong animal lover, cat rescuer, and U.S. Marine veteran. He publishes the animal news website 4PawNews.com and is the former publisher of the animal welfare newspaper—*The New York Companion*. A proud NYC native, Michael now resides in upstate NY with his beautiful wife and two amazing, animal-loving sons. The author attributes all his accomplishments to the guidance, sacrifice, and love given by his parents, Timothy Mullins and Theresa Cummings, and his grandmother, Rose Marsico-Cummings.